SOLDIERS FROM THE HILLS: THE GURKHAS

By
Lieutenant Colonel A.J. Ferrea

U.S. Army War College
Carlisle Barracks, Pennsylvania 17013

23 March 1988

ABSTRACT

AUTHOR: A.J. Ferrea, LTC, AV
TITLE: Soldiers from the Hills, The Gurkhas
DATE: 23 March 1988

The Gurkha regiments in the British Army are among the world's finest infantrymen. Recruited in the kingdom of Nepal since 1819, they have served the kings and queens of Britain with loyalty and incredible bravery. Their battle cry "Here comes the Gurkhas!" has caused enemy soldiers to flee the battlefield and has given the Gurkha a combat potential far greater than his numbers.
The Gurkha soldier has fought beside his British brothers in arms in the Indian Mutiny, in France and Mesopotamia during World War I, and in all theaters during World War II. They have fought as well in Britain's countless small wars including the Northwest Frontier of India, Malaya, Borneo, and in 1982 the Falkland Islands. Like the French Foreign Legion the Gurkhas courage is legendary. Since 1911, when they became eligible, thirteen Gurkhas have been awarded the Victoria Cross. This work will tell you who the Gurkhas are, and where they came from. It will describe their customs, character and their history as soldiers with some reasons why they are among the world's best soldiers.

The views expressed in this paper are those of the author and do not necessarily reflect the views of the Department of Defense or any of its agencies. This document may not be released for open publication until it has been cleared by the appropriate military service or government agency.

SOLDIERS FROM THE HILLS, THE GURKHAS.

At exactly 3:17 p.m. on 15 March 1985 Captain Rambohadur Limbu, V.C. (Victorian Cross), a legend in his own lifetime, passed through the gates of Queen Elizabeth Barracks, Church Crookham, England, for the very last time. On this, his last day of British Army service, Captain Rambohadur Limbu stood rigidly as a solitary Gurkha piper played "Auld Laug Syne" and his Battalion Commander read messages from the queen and other well wishers from around the world. All members of his battalion, the 10th Princess Mary's own Gurkha Rifles, including his two sons, paid him an emotional and colorful farewell. Captain Limbu, V.C., MVO, the last V.C. holder on active duty, retired from the British Army. Within 24 hours he arrived on his ten acre farm in Nepal, among the Nepalese hill people he had left behind 28 years before.[1]

For 172 years young Gurkhas from Nepal have been coming down from the hills to soldier for the British. In recent years mercenaries have had a bad odor, but the profession is an ancient and enduring one; almost every European power has used them except Switzerland. Switzerland like Scotland, has always been an exporter of mercenaries, and today still supplies the Swiss Guards to the Pope, along with a noticeable representation in the French Foreign Legion.

France's legionnaires are renowned for their toughness and fighting abilities, but are respected, not loved by France. The Gurkhas, too are noted for their toughness and fighting skills, but the British undoubtedly have enormous affection for their loyal Gurkha mercenaries. They are not like other mercenaries, refugees with a slightly shady past, but professionals who love the ancient craft of soldiering in the service of Queen Elizabeth II. To understand the reasoning for this mutual admiration between people, and the reason Gurkhas are among the world's best infantrymen, one must be acquainted with British expansion since the eighteen hundreds. This history is also the story of a way of life for many from Nepal.

THE COUNTRY

Nepal is the home of the Gurkha soldier, but the term Nepal has a very restricted meaning to the Gurkha. To him it means the valley of Nepal, which contains the capital of the country, Katmandu and the old cities of Patan and Bhatgoon, an area roughly 15 miles long and 13 miles wide. A Gurkha living outside the Valley will always say that he comes "from the hills," not from Nepal.[2]

Nepal is an independent kingdom sandwiched between the northeastern borders of India and the mountains of Tibet. It occupies some 56,000 square miles along the Himalayas. About the size of Iowa, Nepal is 520 miles long and about 100 miles wide. This terrain has affected the physical characteristics of the people, giving them a sturdy build and muscular legs. There are less than 200 miles of all weather roads in Nepal, so men and pack animals are the major form of transportation in the hills and the mountains, more men than animals. Outside of Katmandu Valley, high technology is the two trace ox cart. Even in the 1980s, wheeled transport, electricity, window panes, hospitals, telephones, and most tools are unknown to the majority of Nepalese.

From the gigantic Himalaya mountains flow the rivers which further add to the difficulties of travel in the country. With the sole exception of the short rail and road links leading to the southern ramparts which guard the valley, thoroughfares in Nepal are restricted to the rudimentary foot trails which are often interrupted by rivers and streams during heavy rainstorms. This fact of travel must always be kept in mind when you think about traveling in rural Nepal. Travel is further hindered by the lack of maps and the difficulty in calculating distance. Travel time often fluctuates according to the time of day, the season of the year, or the time it takes a wet handkerchief to dry when it's attached to a walking stick and allowed to flutter in the wind.[3]

GURKHAS

What is a Gurkha? This widely known ethnic term is often loosely applied. A clear cut definition is complicated by the fact that not every man from Nepal is a true Gurkha; likewise, there are many thousands of

Gurkhas who are not Nepalese subjects. Perhaps a proper description of a Gurkha is a man from the martial clans of Nepal. In present day language, the term "Gurkha" is applied indiscriminately and inaccurately to the entire population of Nepal, although the name should be applied only to the members of the old state of Goorkha, which forms only a small part of the kingdom of Nepal.

The Gurkhas are divided into various clans and religions. The religious customs of Gurkhas are in many respects based on those of the Hindu system. But with so independent a race, there are customs and ceremonies which are peculiar to Gurkhas. Their dialects vary as much as those in any Eastern European country.

There are nine main tribes of Gurkhas: Thakurs, Chetris, Magars, Gurungs, Tamangs, Limbus, Rais, Sanvars, and Newars. With the exception of the Newars, all of these subgroups have one thing in common: an ancient claim to the bearing of arms and military service. All habitually carry the national weapon, the Kukri, a distinctive curved knife.[4]

The Gurkhas differ considerably in appearance. The Rais have a more typical Mongolian face, whereas the Chetri shows a greater likeness to approximate the Indian. In addition to their own tribal language, all can speak Nepali (the British Army calls it Gurkhali). This is the language that British officers must learn upon assignment to a Gurkha Regiment.

THE NEPAL WAR

At the beginning of the nineteenth century the Nepal frontier stretched for two hundred miles further than it does today. Following several incidents, on 20 May 1814 Gurkha troops of the Nepalese Army attacked three British police posts.

Eighteen policemen were killed, four were wounded, and the police chief was taken prisoner and barbarously executed.[5]

Lord Moira, the Indian Governor General, decided that full scale military action was the only way to bring peace and order along the frontier. He dispatched a force of over thirty thousand men, who were to make a four column attack along the frontier. Before the fighting ended, he had to add another twenty thousand troops, because the twelve thousand Gurkhas proved to be tough and courageous foes, experts in mountain warfare. Further, only one of the four British generals commanding the columns, Major General Octlerlory, had the tactical daring that was needed to do the job. The major battles were fought in the west, where the Gurkha Army was commanded by Kaji Amar Sing Thapa, Governor of the region.[6]

The Gurkhas proved their bravery at Kalunga, an isolated jungle covered hill, five hundred feet high, with a fort of stone and logs at the top. Balbohadur, the nephew of the region's Governor, was in command of six hundred Gurkhas. They kept four thousand British and native troops at bay for thirty three days. When the battle was over, Balbohadur led less than one hundred survivors through the British lines at night.

But the Gurkhas' bravery was not enough. Other battles followed the same pattern. The Gurkha troops fought bravely but were outnumbered and outgunned. The King, Amar Sing, convinced that it would be hopeless to continue the war, asked for terms. By the convention of 15 May 1815, the Gurkhas agreed to give up some territory along the frontier.

The British were so impressed with the Gurkhas' fighting qualities that a Treaty of Friendship was signed with Nepal. Included in this treaty was the offer for Gurkhas to enlist into the British service. The agreement between Nepal and Great Britain permits the recruits to serve as mercenaries who do not lose their Nepalese citizenship, even though they take an oath of allegiance to the crown.[7]

On 24 April 1815 the Governor General authorized the formation of the first Gurkha battalion. The first recruits came from prisoners or war who chose to enter British service. Three battalions were formed, the First and Second Nasiri Battalions and the Sirmoor Battalion. A fourth battalion was formed from the Gorakkpur hill regiments, the Kumaon Provincial Battalion. Within a few years the Second Nasiri Battalion was disbanded. But the others have continued with some little changes to this day. Thus the Gurkhas started their long and trusted association with the British.[8]

During the battle of Sambhar in the Pindari War of 1817 and again in the Mahratta War of 1817-18, the Sirmoor Battalion became the first Gurkha battalion to see action in British service. Elements of both the Sirmoor and Nasiri battalions won the first of many battle honors at the siege of Bhurtpore in 1825-26. For the next twenty years, the Gurkha battalions were employed mostly in chasing bandits, a hard and sometimes bloody job.

THE GREAT MUTINY

In 1857 India was divided into three regions, called presidencies: Madias, Bombay, and Bengal, the largest and most important, included the Punjab. Each had its own army. The great Indian mutiny, which began in Meerut, was confined to the Bengal Army. Everyone liked the New Enfield rifle, but the greased cartridge was a different matter. Rumor had it that the cartridge, which had to be bitten before being loaded into muskets, was greased with a mixture of animal fats, pig fat opposed by Moslems and cow fat repugnant to Hindus. By biting into it the Hindu would lose caste and have to pay for costly purification rites. The Muslim would also be seriously defiled.

The British Indian Army tried to relieve the tension by relaxing the normal drill, permitting the men to use their hands instead of their teeth for tearing off the end of the cartridge. They also allowed Hindu and Moslem units to supply their own grease.

But these concessions had the wrong effect. They were interpreted as confirmation of the rumors and due to the strong religious beliefs; this issue provided the perfect spark for rebellion.

Late Sunday in May 1857, while the British were attending evening church service at Meerut, the Indian army revolted.

They shot their officers, murdered the officer's families, looted the homes and burned all the buildings.

In Bengal there were about 150,000 Indian troops, 1,000 Gurkhas, and 23,000 British soldiers. It was then too late for the British Government to regret their policy of not replacing the British troops dispatched to the Crimea War. After some confusion during the first days of the mutiny, the British began to organize their available forces for an attack on Delhi. In this force was the Sirmoor Battalion of Gurkhas.

Now began what was called the Siege of Delhi. It was not a siege in strict military terms. The British did not have the forces to surround the city, which was seven miles in circumference. Instead, they occupied the key ridge overlooking the city walls and repelled all efforts to dislodge them. From this defensive position, the British force launched attacks on the city's gates. Three months later, the siege ended with a final British push through the Kashmir Gate. The city was taken.

During this operation, ninety Gurkha soldiers were added to the original 490 men of the Sirmoor Battalion. The Gurkhas suffered 327 casualties during the siege. Only one British officer of the nine on hand at the beginning of the battle came through unscathed. The Gurkha Kumaon Battalion also served with distinction in storming the Kashmir Gate. They too suffered heavy casualties.

During the mutiny, no less than six battalions of Gurkhas were called to action. The Gurkha Regiments were the first to take action against the mutineers, standing firm to their oath of allegiance to the crown. This confrontation showed two enduring characteristics of the Gurkha soldier, loyalty and fighting ability. In 1860, in recognition for the service of the Gurkhas during the mutiny, the British returned to Nepal lands taken in 1851.[9]

THE FAR FRONTIER

From the mutiny onwards the Gurkhas steadily expanded until, by the turn of the century, there were ten Gurkha regiments serving the British Crown. The Gurkha units were now removed from the normal numbering of infantry of the line and placed in a separate category. (There was some confusion in following the regiments' history because of the title changes, e.g. the 1st Battalion had ten title changes between 1858 to 1936.) When the Sirmoor Battalion was put on the rolls as a regular rifle unit, it became subject to the rule that rifle regiments do not carry colors. The Sirmoor Battalion had just received official recognition for its services at Delhi and awarded a third color, inscribed as "Delhi." Upon hearing that they could not display their colors, Queen Victoria sent a special mark of favor, the Silver Truncheon, a unique trophy carried on a staff by a Gurkha officer. The Truncheon is accorded the same honors as the Queen's color in line regiments. It was carried in the procession for the coronation of Queen Elizabeth II and afterward a representative party of the regiment took the Truncheon to Buckingham Palace for the Queen's inspection. To commemorate this event, two silver collars were affixed to the staff, inscribed "The Queen Truncheon was carried in procession at her Majesty's Coronation, 2 June 1953." "Inscribed by order of Her Majesty Queen Elizabeth II."[10]

On the Northwest frontier of India, the Gurkhas earned five battle honors in two of the three wars Britain fought against Afghanistan and the warlike Pathan tribes. The Pathans inhabited the territory that separated British India from Afghanistan. The most common duties of troops on the Northwest Frontier was guarding caravans, convoys and other troops by securing the passes through which they traveled. It is rugged, mountainous country with forts made of stone. In fact, every house is a small fortress, complete with tower. The fighting was hard, often at close quarters. The British took few prisoners and the enemy none at all. When a prisoner did fall into the hands of the Pathans, they mutilated them. Slicing their testicles off and stuffing them into their mouths was normal practice. Like American Cavalry troops that fell into the hands of some American Indian tribes, Gurkha luck would sometimes have them die before torture began.

Most of the Gurkha regiments fought on the Northwest Frontier. However, the 5th Gurkhas, served the longest: they stayed for ninety years. The 5th became the most famous and most decorated of all Gurkha regiments. Soldiers of the regiment won seven Victoria Crosses. It was the only Gurkha regiment to be designated 'Royal'. Further, it was allowed to add 'Frontier Force' to its title. That title stayed with the unit until 1947, when the 5th Royal Gurkha Rifles (Frontier Force) left British service and became part of the Indian Army. It was said that the fierce Pathans respected only the Prophet and a Gurkha with a kukri.[11]

THE NORTHEAST FRONTIER

Peace was never permanently established on the Northeast Frontier between India and Burma, as it was on the Northwest Frontier. From 1860 to the end of World War II, a number of Gurkha battalions were assigned in Assam (or Northwest Bengal). The Northeast never enjoyed the romantic images (and later Hollywood movies) that portrayed the Northwest Frontier. Even in World War II the Fourteenth Army, (under General William Slim, a Gurkha officer,) was known as the "forgotten army."

The Northeast tribes were not as blood thirsty or cruel as those on the Northwest Frontier. But the hills and jungles in which they lived and fought were tougher to negotiate than the lands of the Pathans. In the fourteen years prior to World War I, the Gurkhas enjoyed few opportunities for Gurkhas to distinguish themselves in large battles. There were only two military expeditions of any note. One was into

Tibet, and the other was an expedition into the Bazer Valley on the frontier. Tibet was the largest one, and the 8th Gurkhas joined the expedition. The Gurkhas did not add to their battle honors. They did, however, add to their reputation as soldiers. Small men from a small kingdom who would fight and die on many fields, always with honor. The world learned the code of the Gurkhas: "I will keep the faith."[12]

Stories about the Gurkhas's steadfastness, loyalty, and sense of humor began to circulate, first within the Indian army then throughout the Empire. Gurkha stories reveal an old fashioned people used to hardship. One of the frontier stories tells of a Corporal who was cutting scrub wood with his Kukri in order to clear a field of fire for his machine gun. His hand slipped and the Kukri all but severed his left thumb. He looked at his dangling thumb for a moment. Then he bit it off, put it in his pocket, bandaged the stump with a handkerchief, and went on with his business. Later that evening he went to the doctor, pulled the thumb from his pocket and asked, half jokingly, "Can you put this back on for me, Sahib?"[13]

One night on the Northwest Frontier a sentry, after being relieved of his duty, left the stone fort without telling anyone where he was going. Then he went out to use the toilet some twenty yards away. A few minutes later the new sentry saw a dark, armed figure looming out of the night. The sentry took aim and challenged the figure. The figure did not answer, maybe he did not know he was being challenged, and the sentry fired, killing the off duty sentry. The sentry who fired was in due course promoted to Lance Corporal for his alertness. But the problem was that under Hindu rites the body must be burned. But it had been raining off and on for days. A senior non commissioned officer (NCO) was placed in charge of the burning party and issued the necessary wood and oil. Off the party went with the corpse on a mule cart. It was raining and the wood would not ignite. The NCO described what happened. "Old Phanjet kept sitting up as the flames licked him, and raising his arms as if he were saying, this is too damned hot. In the end we had to cut him up and burn him a piece at a time. You've never seen anything so funny!"[14] This is simple Gurkha humor, something any of us might laugh at. Their humor would be needed, for the dogs of war were loose. Soon the Gurkha battalions would be answering the call to arms, World War I (WWI).

WORLD WAR I

The British Expeditionary Force in France was outnumbered and ill equipped for modern war. The Expeditionary Force fought courageously but was barely hanging on. The large Territorial Army of Great Britain was still mobilizing. Fresh troops, hopefully trained, were needed from anywhere to hold the Allied line. The anywhere was India. India had trained British, Indian, and Gurkha regiments with outstanding histories as soldiers.

The Gurkhas were delighted to he going to war, though they had no idea of where they were going or under what conditions they would he fighting. As Hindus they needed a special dispensation because Hindus are forbidden to cross the sea under pain of losing caste. In all cases a purification ceremony, Pani Patiya, was required upon their return from overseas. Nepals's supreme religious authority gave his approval for the Gurkhas to cross the Kala Pani black water.[15]

Many of the Gurkha Battalions were at rest with officers and men on extended leave. All that changed rapidly. The message went out to all corners of India and the distant mountains of Nepal. Within a month the battalions were forming up, ready for shipment to the far war. The Gurkhas had no idea of the cause of the war, nor did they care. Coming from the Kingdom of Nepal with its absolute ruler, they were not accustomed to asking such questions. They fought for their honor and that of the Regiment, for their fellow soldiers, for pay and pension, for the excitement of battle and simply because their officers told them to. Western civilization and/or making the world safe for democracy never entered their minds. In today's complex and materialistic times, such motives may be simple to the point of being ridiculous. But their martial sentiments are real and honest, another reason why they are among the best soldiers in the world.

All the Regiments raised a third battalion during the war with the exception of the 4th and 10th. In addition the 3rd raised a fourth battalion along with a companion Regiment, the llth, which also raised four battalions. Approximately one hundred men per battalion were held as reserves in Nepal. This number proved to be totally inadequate. During the course of the war both the Burma Rifles and Burma Military Police were enlisted in mass as replacements for the regular Gurkha battalions.[16]

The Indian Corps formed, consisting of two divisions: the 7th or Meerut Division and the 3rd or Lahore Division. The troops were a mixture of Sikhs, Jats, Garhwals, Pathans, and British. Each of their brigades had one or more battalions of Gurkhas. The Lahore Division sailed from Karachi on 24 August and reached Marseilles on 26 September. The division left one brigade to guard the Suez Canal, so it did not join the division until November. The Meerut Division left Karachi on 21 September and reached France on 11 October. At the port of embarkation in Karachi, many of the Gurkhas saw the sea for the first time; most had not seen such big ships before. During the voyage some of them were seen hanging over the side. Asked what they were looking, for they answered: "the ship's legs." Others wanted to know where all the water came from and where it went. Still others believed that the ship ran on rails at the bottom of the sea. Otherwise, how could the ship find its way? The sea is not the Gurkhas element. Indeed some became seasick before they left port.

The French in Marseilles turned out to give the Indian Corps a splendid welcome, overwhelming them with kindness. In return, the troops earned the reputation of being the best behaved and the most considerate of all the various armies. In addition, the little brown Gurkhas provided the French women with a good laugh: issued for the first time with warm underwear, they donned them proudly over their outer garments and marched through the streets.[17]

At the end of October most of them went to their deaths in the trenches. Trench warfare was completely foreign to the Gurkhas. It gave them no chance to bring their natural ability into play, as in mountain and jungle operations. Gurkhas are a strong individual, but in this kind of war individual strength did not count for anything. For the first time the Gurkhas had to face the full blast of modern artillery, machine guns, and gas. On top of all these was the physical misery of wet and cold, to which they were unaccustomed. Yet, in spite of these things, they had the courage, tenacity, and adaptability to overcome tremendous difficulties and to achieve a quality of fighting which made them feared by the enemy.

In 1915 at the second battle of Ypres, a wounded British officer of the 1st Battalion, 4th Gurkha Rifles, managed to crawl into a ditch. On the lip of this hole lay a Gurkha rifleman, Moti Lal Thapa, his arm practically severed by a shell splinter. When the second wave of troops approached, the officer had Moti Lal dragged into the ditch and his arm bandaged. The attack passed them by. When no stretcher bearers arrived, the exhausted British officer fell asleep. Moti Lal propped himself against the side of the ditch and held his field service hat so that it kept the sun from his officer's eyes. Unaware of this, the officer slept for a few hours. When he awakened, Moti Ia1 was still holding up the hat. In great pain, he kept saving over and over: "I must not cry out. I am a Gurkha." He died on the way to the aid station.[18] We see here another characteristic of the Gurkha soldier, devotion.

After thirteen months in France, the Indian Corps was withdrawn and the exhausted, battered battalions were sent to fight elsewhere. The Corps had fought well in France, adding to their reputation as outstanding professional soldiers. The Corps had suffered 21,000 casualties and was awarded eight VC. For the first time native born Gurkhas were among those eight. (Indians and Gurkhas of the Indian Army did not become eligible for VC's until October 1911.)

As Byron Farwell records in <u>The Gurkhas</u>, military historians questioned the wisdom of sending the Indian Corps to France. They were inadequately clothed and carried only two machine guns per battalion; they had no mortars and only second rate grenades. They also required special food, and the space on ships for the curry and rice could have been better used. Replacements had to be transported thousand of miles. British officers who understood the Indian Army were hard to replace. The plan to send two divisions to France was a mistake; the decision to withdraw them for use elsewhere was wise. Even so, General Sir James Willcock, Commander of the Indian Corps later said of the Gurkhas: "I have now come to the conclusion that the best of my troops in France were the Gurkhas.

GALLIPOLI

In 1915, plans were drawn to knock Turkey out of the war and open a direct Line of communication with Russia. The plan initially called for taking Gallipoli peninsula, the key to the Dardanelles.

The Commander of British Gallipoli Forces asked specifically for a brigade of Gurkhas to round out the New Zealand Division. He felt that this terrain would allow the Gurkhas to do their best. Four battalions served in the Gallipoli Campaign; three in the 29th Brigade. (The fourth Battalion served in an Indian Brigade.) The brigade consisted of the 1/5th (1st Battalion/5th Regiment), 1/6th, and the 2/10 Gurkhas (when using a slash the Battalion's number is followed by the Regiment's) who arrived five days after the main expeditionary force landed on 25 April 1915. The main force landed at the tip of the peninsula and fifteen miles north on the western side.

The 29th Gurkhas Brigade was in continuous combat, suffering their first casualties within a few hours of landing. To the west of the beachhead was a bluff about 300 feet high. The Turks had converted the bluff into a major strongpoint with machine guns covering all approaches. Two previous attempts to secure the bluff by a British Army battalion and one from the Royal Marines failed. The 1/6 Gurkhas were given the task; they lost no time in attacking the bluff. With speed and uncommon courage the bluff was taken at a cost of eighteen killed and forty two wounded. After the battle a special army order changed the name of the bluff to Gurkhas Bluff.[20]

For the rest of the month action was confined to trench warfare. The Gurkhas conducted many night raids and casualties continued to mount. As the ill fated campaign continued, conditions worsened. Some trenches were only fifty yards from the enemy, and the gap of No Man's Land never exceeded two hundred yards. It was a graveyard of rotting corpses, mostly Turkish. The stench was over powering. Intense heat, flies, lice, and fleas added to the discomfort of the troops.[21] Many of the dead had been buried inside or just outside the trenches. The Gurkhas stuffed their nostrils with rifle bore patches.

During one daylight assault against the Gurkhas' position, the Turks lost over 800 men within fifteen minutes. The rifles of the stocky little men from Nepal became so hot that fresh ones had to be passed forward from supporting trenches. It was estimated that the Turks lost two thousand troops in this attack.

On 9 July 1915 the entire Gurkha Brigade, needing rest and reorganization, was withdrawn to the Isle of Imbras. Since their arrival, the three Gurkha Battalions had suffered over a thousand killed and wounded. The 2/10 lost seventy percent of its officers and forty percent of other ranks, including Staff. Only eight British officers remained in the brigade. By August the campaign had ground down to a complete stalemate. The reinforced Turks began to outnumber the attacking Allies.

So the three Gurkhas battalions were landed once again and took part immediately in an attack against hill Q. In this bloody battle, the 1/6 assumed the main burden. The key to the whole peninsula was in their hands. After three nights and two days of fighting, the Gurkhas held the crest. Then, typical of this campaign, the Royal Navy suddenly opened fire on the crest line held by the Gurkhas. Realizing the British were hombarding their own troops the Turks counterattacked and pushed the 1/6 off the position. By daybreak the 1/6 had lost all of its British officers; command was passed to Subadar-major (Gurkha major) Gambirsing Pun, an outstanding soldier who spoke no English. So all communications to and from higher headquarters had to he translated by the battalions' Indian medical officer.

The hopeless fight dragged on for over three months. To add to the hardship, in November a fierce gale swept across the peninsula battlefield. Rain flooded the trenches and turned every stream into a raging river. A blizzard followed, covering the slopes with snow. In three and a half days two hundred men died from exposure. Ten thousand sick were evacuated. The 2/10 Gurkhas suffered cases of frostbite, and ten men died from the weather. When the weather subsided, the battalion had on strength just over one hundred men. When the battalion arrived from Egypt, it came ashore with thirteen British and seventeen Gurkha officers leading 734 soldiers. When the 2/10 left Gallipoli six months later, its ranks numbered one British officer and seventy nine Gurkha of other ranks. In the twenty one months since leaving India, of the 2404 officers and men serving in the battalion, 1450 became casualties. (The 2404 was broken down as forty two British officers, fifty two Gurkha officers and 2310 other ranks.)

At last just before Christmas 1915 the end came. The British, knowing victory could not be theirs, ordered evacuation. To the 5th Gurkhas went the honor of being the last troops to quit the peninsula. Behind them they left only their dead and a reputation among the Turks for bravery and fighting ability second to none.

General Sir Ian Hamilton, the commander at Gallipoli, who was relieved of his command, had his secretary write to the Colonel of the 6th Gurkha Rifles: "It is Sir Ian Hamilton's most cherished conviction that had he been given more Gurkhas in the Dardanelles then he would never have been held up by the Turks."[22] As the Turks well knew, the 6th had come so near to victory.

SUEZ AND MESOPOTAMIA

The Suez and Mesopotamia (present day Iraq) campaign was an exercise in futility. It cost far more in lives than any tactical value the cities of Kut (Kut-el-Amara) or Baghdad offered. The latter was retaken after the initial British force (including the 2/7 Gurkhas) surrendered under a Turkish siege.

The fate of the world was decided in Europe not in the Near East. For the Allies, the war in Mesopotamia was a sideshow. For Turkey and most Arabs, it was the main event. The main British concern was the protection of the Persian Gulf oilfields, which were never in any real danger. After three years of campaigning, the Mesopotamian operation cost over 90,000 British empire casualties, including nearly 29,000 dead. The Turks lost over 45,000 prisoners and unnumbered dead and wounded. It is hard to justify such heavy casualties in an apparently unnecessary campaign.[23]

All ten Gurkha regiments had one or more battalions in Mesopotamia at some time during the three year war. The fighting took place in a loand that was barren and most inhospitable, but again the Gurkhas increased their reputation is good soldiers, particularly as good infantrymen, who could endure pain and physical hardship.

Stories of their obedience to orders and never failing good humor were rampant in the campaign. Two examples: A British warship, lights out, armed with 6 and 3 inch guns, moved slowly up the heavily defended Suez Canal early in 1915. The officer on watch heard a small voice shouting from the land. He understood the voice to be saying, "Halt! Who go dah?" The officer did not reply. The voice then said, "Halt or I fire!" The ship turned on a searchlight, which illuminated one Gurkha rifleman standing on the bank. His rifle was pointed at the bridge. The ship stopped; its captain sent an urgent message for help. So the officer of Gurkhas was found to tell the sentry that the ship could pass. The Gurkha then shouted, "pass friend, all's well," and lowered his rifle. The ship glided on, with the British crew laughing and cheering.

A machine gun team of the 4th Gurkhas was in action in Mesopotamia when the number 1 gunner was shot in the head. He was quickly replaced by the number 2 gunner, but he too was shot. Then number 3 moved forward to man the gun and he was in turn shot. There was a burst of laughter from his comrades in a nearby trench. They had made a bet on the number 3 gunner's chances of survival. The winner was entirely jubilant. [24]

The Gurkha battalions served with distinction in France, Gallipoli, and Palestine. Like the France Foreign Legion, Gurkhas were now considered a Corps d'elite. Their reputation ensured that each battalion would be equipped the same as their British Army counterparts in light infantry battalions and that only above average officers would be selected to serve with them.

In WWI Nepal put at the disposal of the British Government all the manpower resources of the country. The British gratefully accepted and used Nepalese troops to garrison India. Britain also called upon Nepal to render assistance in recruiting for the maintenance of Gurkha regiments of the Indian Army and for additional battalions for those regiments. During WWI over 200,000 Gurkhas joined the British services; 55,000 of these were enlisted in the regular battalions. Their casualties totaled 20,000, more than the strength of the entire Gurkha Brigade before the war.

BETWEEN THE WARS

The years between the two world wars provided no peaceful period of rest. While European and the American armies were being demobilized in 1919, all ten Gurkha regiments were engaged on the Northwest Frontier of India as were three battalions of the 11th, raised for the war. The 11th did not remain for long after the armistice.

The new intake of young subalterns after the war were for the most part Lieutenants who served in combat with British regiments of the Territorial Army. These regiments were demobilized and reverted to reserve status. The many officers and few non-commissioned officers who wanted to remain on active duty had to find regiments. Most of these officers were from low income families and had no second income, which was needed to live in almost all British regiments of the line. The British Indian Army gave them the opportunity they sought. Those with outstanding war records, good education, and a desire to serve were selected for the Gurkha regiments. Among them was

Lieutenant William J. Slim from the Warwickshire Regiment. He later became Field Marshal Slim, commander of the Fourteenth Army in Burma during World War II. He watched the 1/6 at Gallipoli and was so impressed he joined the Regiment.

The Gurkhas fought in Waziristan in 1919, on the Malabar coast in 1921-22, in Waziristan again in 1925, and in Burma in 1930-32. There was little time to relax. During this period the face of war changed. Aircraft and armor and other new weapons were assimilated into the traditional methods of frontier warfare, at which the Gurkhas excelled. Would they adapt to more technical warfare? Their chance to fight a modern war came soon enough.

WORLD WAR II

The complexities of World War II make it impossible to follow in detail the activities of the ten regiments of Gurkha Rifles. Only the most important events will be discussed. The war came slowly to the British Indian Army. While Britain and the commonwealth mobilized their manpower, India, a major source of trained soldiers in the first World War, did not begin its military expansion until almost a year after the German Armies crossed the Polish frontier. In the first two years of the conflict, the Indian Army was asked for only two divisions to serve outside of India.

As in the past, in 1939 Nepal came forward with offers of assistance even before the actual declaration of war. This offer was refused. Another year would pass before the British asked the Maharaja for help. Sir Judha Shamsher Jamg Brahadur Rana, the Maharaja, proved himself a staunch ally of Great Britain. Early in 1940 two brigades of four battalions each were dispatched to India: one went to Kakul, and the other to Dehra Dum. Throughout the war, most of the Contingent was kept fully occupied on the Northwest Frontier, where they performed their duties with zeal and enabled battalions of the Indian Army to fight elsewhere. Three battalions fought in the Japanese campaign in Assam and Burma, where they further enhanced the Gurkha reputation. In addition, two pioneer battalions were dispatched for work in Assam and on the Ledo road in Burma.

In 1940 the Maharaja authorized raising a third battalion and shortly afterward, a fourth battalion, for each of the ten regular regiments of the Gurkha Brigade. Two further regiments were raised for the duration of the war, the 25th and 26th (these were disbanded shortly after peace was declared).[25]

NORTH AFRICA

The Italian government's entrance into the war on 10 June 1940 presented no immediate threat to Britain's position in Africa and the Mediterranean. Although British forces were outnumbered by more than two to one (by three to one in Armor), they succeeded in thoroughly mauling their adversaries and inflicting heavy losses in manpower and equipment. But in March, Hitler sent General Erwin Rommel and his Panzer Afrika Korps to North Africa. At once he began an attack that drove the British back to Tobruk. Finally stopped at El Alamein, Rommel again attacked, taking his panzers on a wide sweep south into the desert and swinging north inside the British lines.

The British Eighth Army retreated and again Tobruk was isolated. Churchill demanded another stubborn defense, but conditions had changed. Tobruk fell on 21 June. Captured in the debacle was the 11th Indian Brigade, which included the 2/5 and 2/7 Gurkhas, who had not received word of the surrender and who fought on for thirty six hours longer, until their water and ammunition were finished and they could fight no more. History has a habit of repeating itself. So it was with the 2/7 Gurkhas.

For the second time, this battalion had been captured, at Kut-el-Amara in the First World War and now at Tobruk. In both instances it was reformed and lived on to fight in the same brigade of the 4th Indian Division.

Stories of Gurkhas began to circulate in North Africa. One concerned a German officer who took cover in a dugout during a British artillery barrage at the start of the battle for Tobruk. When the battle ended, he started to come out, only to see the advancing Indians. So he dived into hiding again. He remained for some hours, fearing that if he was caught behind the British lines he might be executed as a spy. In the end hunger drove him out. In broad daylight, in full uniform with hands raised, he walked boldly down the road to Tobruk, where he was officially taken prisoner. The British asked it he met any of their troops on his way to Tobruk. The German replied, "Oh, yes. Many of them. But they were Gurkhas and they all saluted me!"[26]

Many of the captured 2/5 and 2/7 managed to escape. Some made it back to friendly lines. Havildar (Sergeant) Kharkabahadur Rai of the 2/7 soon escaped after his capture at Tobruk. But was recaptured and sent to Italy. After fifteen months he escaped again and lived in the mountains for three months before he was captured once more. This time the Germans sent him to Germany and then to southern France. Here he escaped for the third time. In southern France he joined a band of Maquis led by an American OSS Colonel and fought with them until American troops reached the area. Kharkabahadur Rai was sent to Paris and then to London. From there, at the end of the war, he returned to his regiment.

ITALY

All Gurkha regiments except the second sent battalions to fight in Italy as part of the British Eight Army. During the fighting around the vicinity of Cassino, a patrol went out to locate German positions. After slipping by two enemy sentries in the dark, they found another four Germans asleep in a barn. The Germans were sleeping in a row. Using their Kukri, the Gurkhas beheaded two men. But left the other two to wake up and try to rouse their comrades. It was a brilliant use of psychological warfare. This kind of calling card let the Germans know who they were facing and that the Germans could not hide.

After Cassino, the Gurkhas took part in the rush towards the Gothic Lines. By the end of July 1944 they were in the Arno valley. The fighting continued until 2 May 1945, when the German Army in Italy surrendered. For the Gurkhas it was the end of a long bitter and bloody campaign. They had won the admiration of friend and foe alike. Soon after the surrender, they would be homeward bound. But they would leave behind many comrades who had fought and died in this land called Italy. All who come in contact with the Gurkhas would remember these stocky little men from Nepal whose motto "KAPHAR HUNNU BHANDA MARNU RAMO" (It is better to die than to be a coward)[27] gave them a combat potential far greater than their numbers.

BURMA

For the Gurkhas, the war in Southeast Asia must be divided into two halves: The retreat from Burma and the hard bloody road back. The Gurkhas played a prominent role in this theater. All ten regiments were represented, with more than 20 battalions engaged in the fighting.

After being pushed out of Burma and with only limited resources available for Southeast Asia, the British, despite their strategic priorities, could make no more than a tentative stab eastward. Lieutenant General Sir William Slim Commander of the 14th Army, had a monumental task before him, getting the defeated troops into fighting trim. This he did.

CHINDITS

Gurkhas history in World War II would he incomplete without mentioning the Chindits, Long Range Penetration Groups (LRP) of the sometimes remarkable Brigadier Orde Wingate. Brig. Wingate derived this name from the Burmese "chinths," a lion or the Griffith-like beasts that sometimes adorn pagodas. Wingate, who had given the Italians a hard time in Ethiopia, advocated landing Large forces behind enemy lines. They would harass enemy lines of communications and disrupt logistical networks. His first expedition in 1942 was badly organized, ineffective and costly. The group could not be evacuated by air and had to make it out in small groups; over one third of the original force did not survive. The 3/2nd and 3/6th Gurkha battalion took part in this expedition. Wingate, an artillery officer who once attempted suicide, was unfamiliar with the Indian Army. Except from their reputation he was ignorant of Gurkhas. Militarily the operation had been a failure. But psychologically it had made the Japanese worry about rear area security.

With increased air transport capability and improved techniques, Wingate was ready to try again. The second Chindits penetration was made by five infantry brigades organized as the 3rd Infantry Division. Within this force were five Gurkha battalions: the 3/2nd and 3/6th were joined by 3/4th, 3/9th, and 4/10th. The initial invasion was by glider onto two isolated jungle locations. The Chindit columns did not accomplish enough to justify the effort. Once again casualties were high. The troops suffered greatly.

On March 25 Wingate was killed in a B25 bomber crash in Western Burma. General Slim replaced him with Brigadier Lentaigh, a British Gurkha officer whose 111th Brigade was blocking the main railroad line. Lentaign's replacement for the 111th Brigade was another Gurkha officer, Major (promoted to Brigadier) John Masters, who conducted a fighting withdrawal to safety at Mokso Sakkan. Masters, the professional Gurkha officer, brought out with him 130 wounded and 2,000 men "organized and under arms."[28]

During WW II only one hundred Victoria Crosses were awarded; thirty one were given to men who fought in Burma. Of the one hundred VC in WW II, twelve were won by Gurkhas, along with 2,734 other awards. The Gurkhas' price in casualties totaled 23,655, including 7,544 killed in action.[29]

With the war's end many Gurkha battalions were placed on occupation duty. The four battalions sent to Siam (present Thailand) had no great problems with the Japanese. The Japanese Army gave no trouble whatsoever. They had been told to surrender and they did. The Japanese retained control over their organization. Orders were given to their officers, who saw that they were carried out. Their discipline was good and all tasks were carried out promptly. Not even when officers' personal swords were collected did their faces show any sign of emotion. The Gurkhas, no strangers to casual sex, found venereal disease a major problem to which they fell victim in appalling numbers.

This was the only threat the battalions faced while in Thailand. After much difficulty, volunteers were found who would demonstrate the proper fitting of the army issued condom.

The 2nd Battalion of the 5th Royal Gurkha Rifles (Frontier Force) was selected to be part of occupational forces in Japan.

The main occupational force would be American, but a British Commonwealth Force would assist them. This consisted of contingents of British, Australian, New Zealand, and Indian troops. All British and Indian contingents came from units in India; they were formed in a Division known as "Brindin". The Commonwealth forces would have to bear comparison with their American Allies. All clothing and equipment, with the exception of American grenade launchers, was to be of British manufacture, generously, indeed lavishly, dispersed. At first the men were a little bewildered at being issued knives, forks, and spoons; razors, shaving brushes and combs. Most Gurkhas have little or no facial hair; they pluck out with tweezers any odd whisker that appears. Until 40 Years ago, Army regulations required that all Gurkhas shave their heads except for a topknot. Gurkhas now are permitted to wear their hair at normal length. Four tailors from Bombay were kept busy for several weeks making new uniforms for the 5th Battalion. As one officer said, "It was a dream come true."[30] So by the end of WW II, Gurkhas had finally been introduced to modern military amenities and logistics!

PARTITION

In 1947 Pakistan and India opted to go their separate ways. The ruling British Labour Government of the time, in a gesture of unparalleled irresponsibility, gave India and Pakistan their freedom without adequate arrangements having been made for the protection of minorities. The total count of casualties will never be known, but estimates indicate two million deaths in Hindu-Moslem conflicts marked by medieval cruelty. Also, Indian princes, who had treaties with the British Government guaranteeing their rights and status, were abandoned to their fate.

In March 1947 Lord Mountbatten, the Viceroy of India, announced the establishment of India and Pakistan as of August 16th. Surely these political changes would affect the Gurkha regiments, but just what would happen was uncertain. Even as late as June the Gurkhas knew nothing of their fate. It was an unsettling and disheartening experience for them, especially as most of the men had little understanding of the intricate political situation.

At Partition the great Indian Army had not yet been divided into its three parts. The Pakistani and Indian governments were to establish a Joint Defense Council on 11 August 1947, and under this Council, Field Marshal Auchinleck was designated the Supreme Commander. His headquarters would continue until 1 April 1948 after which two armies were to be created. However, in November 1947, Auchinleck announced that his headquarters would close for lack of cooperation and goodwill on the part of representatives of the two countries.

Muslim units could not be trusted to guard Hindus, and Hindu units could not be trusted to guard Muslims. Likewise Sikh soldiers killed Muslims they were sent to protect. In such a world only the British and Gurkha battalions could he relied upon. Gurkhas, although Hindus, dealt even handedly and impartially with all, in spite of the tremendous pressures put upon them by Nepalese and Indian politicians.

The Gurkha soldiers were ill rewarded for their steadfast loyalty in those trying days. For the first time since 1816 they were involved in a conflict in which their own interests were at stake. No one knew what was to become of the Gurkha mercenaries.

Being Hindu, it was never contemplated that any of the Gurkha battalions would become part of the Pakistani Army. The question was how many, it any, would stay in the Army of the new India, and how many, if any, would the British retain.

The details of the agreement between India and Great Britain are unknown. But the commanders of the ten Gurkha regimental centers were called to Delhi and told that of the twenty seven active battalions only eight would remain with the British. The rest would he turned over to India. To the frustration and confusion of the commanders, they were not told which battalions would go and which would stay.

At last, on 8 August, the long awaited message was received. The 2nd, 6th, 7th, and 10th Gurkha Regiments had been selected for continued service with the British. The remainder would serve the Indian Government. Precisely why these four regiments would remain with the British is also unknown. However some unit histories suggest that, since all four had battalions in Burma, the selection was made merely on the basis of administrative convenience, because these battalions would not be required to return to India. In addition, the 7th and 10th Gurkhas recruited from eastern Nepal and the 2nd and 6th from western Nepal. This geographic circumstance may have had a major influence on the selection. After partition the Indians raised a new regiment, the 11th Gurkhas, which was recruited in eastern Nepal. Neither British nor Indians changed the regimental numbers. So to this day they are numbered from one to eleven without regard to the country they serve, as if all are still serving one nation.

In the absence at accurate information, rumors filled the vacuum. The most repeated rumor was that Indian officers would soon he assigned to Gurkha battalions. Officers and men in Gurkha battalions considered themselves a cut above the Indian, better than others, superior to most units. There was some warrant for this attitude. Gurkhas were not serially numbered with other regiments of the Indian Army. For all military tasks, Gurkha and British troops were regarded as interchangeable. British Pommies and Johnny Gurkhas fraternized in a way that Indian and British troops never did.

Finally, a referendum was held in each battalion selected to become part of the British regular army. Each Gurkha was given the choice: he could elect to stay with his battalion, transfer to a battalion which would become part of the Indian Army, or take a discharge with some compensation. Most Gurkhas were familiar with India, their families were already there, and India seemed to offer more opportunities for them. Most stayed.

British officers of the battalions that were to be part of the Indian Army had some options: To join a British Gurkha battalion if there were vacancies; to resign within a year and receive 3,300 pounds (in 1947 the pound was worth $4.80) in compensation plus a pension 330 pounds per year; or to transfer to the British Army.[31]

India apparently chose their officers for the Gurkha battalions with great care. All were professional and most were tactful. Tact could and did ease the social strains, but for many the experience remained bitter. Not all British officers behaved decently.

Perhaps the greatest change in the Gurkha units was in names. Since the Viceroy was gone, the British could no longer have Viceroy's Commissioned officers, so all became either Gurkha Commissioned Officers (GCO) or King (later Queen) Gurkha officers. In the Indian Army, the Gurkha officers became Junior Commissioned Officers (JCO). For the Gurkha non-commissioned officers going to the British Army, the ranks were the same as used in that army.

The spelling of the regiments which remained in India was changed to Gorkha; so the 8th Gurkha Rifles, for example, became the 8th Gorkha Rifles. The reason for this is that the principality of Gorkha, from which the Gurkha gets his name, is always spelled with "0". Gurkha is a British derivation.

Since the division of the old Gurkha Brigade, the Indian regiments have played an important part not only in local actions but in world affairs. In 1961 when the Congo was split by rebellion, the 3/1st Gorkha Rifles and the 2/5th Gorkha Rifles were sent to Katanga as part of the United Nations Forces.

MALAYA AND BORNEO

Soon after the Brigade of Gurkhas moved to its new station in Malaya (with Battalions in Hong Kong), the Chinese Communist terrorists launched their campaign of violence in Malaya. Their main targets were isolated rubber estates and tin mines. Many plantation managers and workers were murdered. The Army was called in to deal with the mounting wave of violence, which was threatening Malaya's economic stability. Individual battalions were assigned to large areas with orders to seek out and destroy the terrorist bands.

For twelve years, until the end of the declared state of emergency, the Gurkhas and their British officers performed the most exhausting and heartbreaking tasks with efficiency and cheerfulness. Penetrating into the jungle, sometimes for weeks at a time, they searched for the terrorists' camps, laid ambushes and gradually destroyed the fugitive enemy. While on these grueling operations, they were constantly exposed to the sniper's bullet or sudden ambush from the dense brush. The mental and physical strain was severe. Such operations demanded much patience at all levels, including the senior commanders back at headquarters who were controlling and coordinating the operations.

A good illustration of this patience occurred in 1956. In the area of Segamat in Malaya, one of the most wanted bandits (communist terrorists) was Goh Sia, a ruthless leader who had led a platoon against the Japanese during WW II, before becoming a thorn in the side of the British. The Malayan Government put a price of $35,000 on his head, but even that sum did not bring information of his whereabouts. At last, eight years after the start of the Emergency, credible intelligence led to a small ambush patrol, sent off under the command of Corporal Partapsing Rai of the 1/7th Gurkha Rifles. For three days and nights the Corporal and five riflemen lay hidden in a small patch of tall grass in the middle of a rubber tree plantation. It was an exhausting vigil. The patrol got no protection from the sun by day or shelter from the rain and the damp cold of the night.

Cooking was not possible, nor could the men move out of the patch to answer nature calls because, during the day, rubber tappers worked near the spot most of the time. Even Partapsing had begun to give up hope when, at about nine o'clock in the morning of the third day, Goh Sia appeared on his own and nonchalantly strolled toward the place where food had been left for him by the tappers.

On command of the Corporal, one rifleman shot him. The bandit was killed outright, his terrorist days were over. Only highly trained soldiers could have endured the ordeal needed for this successful ambush. Patience and self discipline of the Gurkha soldier brought about the death of Goh Sia.

The Gurkha is the ideal jungle fighter. He has natural instincts of the countryman, has undergone realistic jungle training and possesses the endurance to keep going hour after hour, if necessary day after day, through back breaking terrain. Size is not important, but physical stamina is.

BORNEO

On Saturday 7 December 1962, the 1/2nd Gurkhas stationed in Singapore were undergoing their Annual Administrative Inspection (AAI). The inspection was not going well, and many were hoping that something would happen as a diversion to the inspection.

That something was an attempted overthrow of the Sultan of Brunei. Revolutionaries, bent on creating an independent state in Northern Borneo, attacked the Sultan's palace, the prime minister's house, the police station, and other important places in the capital city. Although unsuccessful, the rebels had managed to seize the power station and had taken some fifty Europeans as hostages.

At five o'clock in the morning, the Gurkha Brigade alerted the 1/2nd Gurkhas to be ready to send two companies and a tactical headquarters to Brunei as soon as possible. The 1st Battalion was not excited by this order, thinking it was part of the AAI. But gradually a sense of reality emerged as reports of the fighting in Brunei came in.

All that could go wrong did. Trucks that were sent to the ammunition depot were told to come back on Monday. The Brigade map officer was swimming at the beach, but no one knew which beach. There was no transport available to move the troops to the airfield. The Royal Air Force had no aircraft available, and it would take some time before they would be arriving.

In spite of all these difficulties, the Gurkhas arrived at the airfield. After a four hour wait, they took off at five o'clock in the afternoon. By the following morning the 1/2nd had set up its headquarters in the Brunei police station and sent out patrols. The rest of the Battalion arrived that afternoon and immediately located the Sultan, placing him under the hattalion's protection. The next day the hostages were freed.

The Brunei revolt finally collapsed when the last hard core rebels were killed or captured by the 2/7th Gurkhas in a fight on 18 May 1963 a few miles outside Brunei town. However, a month earlier Indonesia began its "confrontation" with Malaysia with an attack on a Sarawak police station. Hostile operations on the part of the Indonesians kept the British Brigade of Gurkhas and Commonwealth troops on combat duty in Borneo for almost four years. Hon. Captain GC0 (Gurkha Commissioned Officer) Limber, won his VC at Serikin, Sarawak, in November 1965, when he was a lance corporal. He joined the Army in 1957 and was commissioned in 1977. We noted his retirement at the outset of this work.

On 1 January 1963, a Gurkha Independent Parachute Company was raised in Malaysia from men in the 7th and 10th Gurkhas for use in Brunei. From this unit comes one of the most often told stories about Gurkhas. A British officer was explaining that jumps were made first from balloons, and later from an airplane at a safe height of a thousand feet or more. The officer was surprised that the Gurkhas looked glum, "1000 feet" said a lance corporal "was a little high, could they not jump at a more reasonable height of 300 feet." The officer explained that at that height their parachutes would not have time to open. "Oh!" said the lance corporal, "we will have parachutes? That's different."[34]

THE FALKLANDS

On the morning of 3 April 1982, the Prime Minister, Thatcher, announced that one British Government had decided to send a task force to the South Atlantic to retake the Falkland Islands. The Islands had been seized by the Argentina Armed Forces on the day before, after a four hour fight by its Royal Marine garrison.

The 1/7 Duke of Edinburgh's own Gurkha Rifles was part of the reconstituted 5th Infantry Brigade. After intensive training in Wales, the 1/7 Gurkha Rifles embarked at Southampton on the *Queen Elizabeth II* on 12 May. After a two and a half week voyage and continuous training on board, the Battalion transferred to MV *Norland* at Grytviken, South Georgia Island. With the remainder of the Brigade on SS *Canberra,* 1/7 Gurkha Rifles then sailed to the Falkland islands on 29 May. An extremely rough three days voyage, not enjoyed by the Gurkha soldiers, ended with the *Norland*, which had taken part in the initial landings of 3 Commando Brigade, being the first ship of 5th Infantry Brigade to sail in San Carlos Water. "D" Company reinforced the bridgehead on the Sussex Mountains. The remainder of the Battalion was flown in the one surviving Chinook helicopter to Darwin and Goose Green. The Battalion spent a week at those locations. Mounting a large number of patrols, they captured ten Argentines. They also assisted in mopping up Goose Green Settlement after the Argentinian occupation and the 2nd PARA Battle.

On 8 June, the Battalion deployed by helicopter to the area of Bluff Cove. "D" Company saw action during the air attacks on the ships *Sir Galahad* and *Sir Tristam*, engaging the attacking aircraft with machine gun and rifle fire.

The Battalion, less "C" Company who were garrisoning Goose Green, subsequently advanced eastwards Wether Ground near Mount Harriet. Occupying positions there, they came under intensive and accurate fire from enemy artillery. By good fortune, only four casualties were taken in this three day period.

On the afternoon of 13 June, the Gurkhas moved again, this time to an area just below the Two Sisters feature. They took part in the 5th Infantry Brigade attack on the final ring of high ground overlooking Port Stanley. On the next morning, the Gurkhas suffered eight more casualties from heavy shelling of the Battalion's advanced position north of the Tumbledown hills, prior to its assault on Mount William. The Argentines, however, much to the Gurkha riflemen's disgust, fled from this position, demoralized by the intensive artillery fire and the knowledge that they were facing the much feared Gurkha kukris. The battle was not joined and soon the Argentines surrendered.

One Gurkha junior NCO was killed by mines; a total of twenty were wounded in the Falkland operation. From the Battalion's point of view, it was a privilege to have taken part in such a highly successful operation. Luck and a good final battle plan played their part in the low casualties.

However, there is no doubt that 1/7 Gurkha Rifles played an important part in bringing hostilities to a speedy conclusion.[35]

When London decided to use the Gurkhas as part of the 5th Brigade, they sent a message to Nepal stating their intentions. The Nepalese government was puzzled by the British message. After all, the Gurkhas were soldiering for the British for well over 17 years. Why ask Nepal for permission for their use now?

BRITISH ARMY RECRUITING

There are still a few soldiering opportunities open for young men raised in the hills of Nepal far from the nearest town. The land cannot provide them all enough of a living. Many must eventually seek work in the world beyond the mountains. For generations this has meant soldiering. Soldiering has provided the one way out of the restricted life of villages.

For the Brigade of Gurkhas there are now three intakes a year from mid February until mid March. In one intake as many as 600 potential recruits come in from the hills. Some have walked for ten days to reach the British Army Depot at Oharan Nepal.

This is the first time most of them have ever left home. For the duration of the recruiting, the potential soldiers are known only by numbers which are painted on their chests and hacks. This lessens the chance of tribal or family favoritism.

Recruits stay at Oharan for twelve days. During that time they will be tested both mentally and physically. Out of an intake of six hundred the British may accept less than half.

Gurkhas are small men, but recruits must weigh at least 105 pounds and be over 5 feet 2 inches tall. Eighteen is the minimum age, but in Nepal there are no birth certificates. So if they look eighteen, they are eighteen. Among the physical tests taken is the British Army fitness test. A recruit jags 1 1/2 miles, followed by a 1 1/2 mile race.

The young men are driven by the knowledge that the reward for success is a chance to see the world, to secure an income, and the prestige of being a British soldier. Many recruits hope for a place in their fathers' and grandfathers' regiments. They know that if they are selected, they will he respected in Nepal as men who have a knowledge of things which those who remain behind will never have. If they fail, they may never get another chance.

After each days' competition the recruiters, "Galah Wallahs," some 40 former senior non-commissioned officers who have walked the Nepalese hills looking for recruits, encourage their groups to keep trying until the testing is over. All 600 potential recruits have two interviews with British officers during their stay at Oharan. These interviews are an important part of the selection process.

The young Gurkhas are naturally competitive, but the British Army needs and wants men who also work well together as a team. They want men who are naturally resilient. During "Murder Ball" no rules soccer, the men who like being in the action show up. The recruiting officers look for those qualities that have made the Gurkha soldier famous. The Brigade of Gurkhas need top men who can endure hardship, who are disciplined, and who follow their motto, "Kaphar Hunnu Bhanda Marnu Ramo" (It is better to die than to be a coward).

Today's recruits, however, have modern technology and equipment to contend with. Those selected are likely to be the ones who have done well in education and intelligence tests, as well as having scored high in the physical competitions. More of today's recruits are "line boys." This term goes back more than a century. In the British Indian Army, each regiment established its own home in India, a cantonment where married men could bring their wives and raise their children. Sons born within the lines of the regiment are called "Line Boys."[36] Until the mid sixties there was a distinct prejudice against them. Most had some schooling in India, Nepal or the British Army school system in Hong Kong. British officers regarded them as "too clever" and much preferred the semi-illiterate hillmen. Today riflemen must have more education than their fathers and grandfathers. Formerly it was not uncommon to have recruits who had only seen Nepal when they traveled to the Recruiting Depot. But now the more sophisticated line boys are more attractive to recruiters. For those who have not been selected, there is little the recruiting officers could advise. The rejected recruits are told to try again next year. Some will not be able to return home with abandoned dreams, they know there is little future for them in the hills. They must seek work elsewhere. The British have paid them for their time, given them a meal and sent them on their way. For those who still want to soldier, there is the opportunity in the Indian or Nepalese armies, where the rejection rite is not so high.

Successful recruits face six busy days before they leave for Hong Kong. Many of their old ways must be put aside and new ones learned. They learn to put on socks, it's easier if you sit down, the right foot first, and lace up boots. Also they get their first military haircut, along with demonstrations on how to eat using a knife, fork and spoon. In addition, some elementary drill is given so when the young soldiers swear allegiance before the Depot priest they will not make fools of themselves. On their last day at the depot, they swear allegiance to the British Crown: "I do swear that I will serve loyally in the Army of Her Majesty the Queen and her Ministers of the British Government. This I do promise in thought, in word, in deed."

After the initial processing at the Depot the recruits are transported to Kathmandu, where they board a Royal Nepalese or RAF aircraft to Kai Tak airport, Hong Kong, overcoming one ordeal by flying in an aircraft, which many had never seen before. Indeed many have never known any form of transportation but the yak and their own two feet. They are now ready for the hustle of Hong Kong. They have little time to see Hong Kong before boarding buses that take them deep into the New Territories to the Training Depot Brigade of Gurkhas (TDBG) at Sek Kong.

After pouring off buses at Sek Kong, they get a meal of bhat, curried vegetables and meat, and mountains of rice. They will never tire of this diet, which they will get twice daily throughout their recruit training. The attrition rate of recruits during basic training is very low. From an intake of 500, the Brigade may lose only two, and this is normally for medical reasons. For the past 3000 recruits the Brigade has lost just eleven men.

Their formal training begins with two weeks of instruction on the Gurkha way of life and discipline modeled after British military manuals. Then they embark on 40 weeks of basic training. The first phase consists of 28 weeks of individual training, after which the recruits will be formed into sections to learn small unit tactics. The individual syllabus consists of periods of training in weapons, the recruits spends 25 days and eight nights on the 30 meter range alone, physical fitness, and drill, along with such non-syllabus matters as the use of electric lights, wearing western clothes, telling time in English, and using flush toilets. In basic training, they are not allowed to smoke, drink, watch television, or go out on pass. All recruits are taught to swim. Because of the Brigade of Gurkhas' role in Hong Kong, they learn the skills of internal security.[37]

Virtually everything is new to them, even such a basic item as a boot. Recruits' feet are not accustomed to such footwear. So much of the physical fitness training is devoted to breaking in both feet and boots. During this period the young recruits receive their kukri, the distinct curved knife which is made by one expert in Sharan Nepal. It is used by all Gurkha troops as an essential part of their equipment. At the completion of the last 14 weeks of training, the recruit will be capable of using all platoon weapons with skill.[38]

All recruits are enlisted initially into the Brigade of Gurkhas. Allocations to infantry regiments and the three Corps units take place during weeks 35 and 36. Direct family claims (such as where father or brother is serving) and area of origin are taken into account. The men from the west will go to the 2nd King Edward VII's Own Gurkha Rifles (The Sirmoor Rifles) and 6th Queen Elizabeth's Own Gurkha Rifles. Those from the east will go to the 7th Duke of Edinburgh's Own Gurkha Rifles and 10th Princess Mary's Own Gurkha Rifles. Half of the recruits for the Queen's Gurkha Engineers, Queen's Gurkha Signals and Gurkha Transport Regiment are taken from each area.

All recruits, whether destined for the infantry or the corps, are trained up to full riflemen standard, so no continuation training has to be carried out by the battalions. Trade training for the Corps units is carried out by their parent Corps after recruit training. During the training cycle, the recruits are taken on organized shopping sprees outside the training camp. (All will wear their regimental blazers with white shirt and regimental tie.)

A young recruit earns $1,000 Hong Kong dollars (HKD) a month, but will only have $100 HKD dollars to spend each month. The rest of their pay is invested for them. This $1,000 (HKD) includes the British supplemental. Under terms of an agreement signed with India the pay for Gurkhas are the same but Great Britain pays a "Gurkha Addition" for both single and married soldiers.

A Gurkha's initial tour of duty with the British Army is four years with no leave. Almost all recruits sign on for 15 years and most will serve the full period. If he signs for a further period, however, he is sent back home for six months leave after three years service. Fifteen years is the minimum for a pension. At the end of that time, anyone below the rank of corporal will be discharged.

The training depot was formed at Sungei Patani in North Malaya in August 1951 to train recruits for the Gurkha rifle regiments which had become part of the British Army in 1947. Before that, each regiment trained its own recruits. As the Gurkha Corps units (Gurkha Engineers, Gurkha Signals, Gurkha Army Service Corps now the Gurkha Transport Regiment, and the now disbanded Gurkha Military Police) were formed, it assumed responsibility for training their recruits as well. In June 1971, after withdrawal of British troops from Malaya and Singapore, the Depot moved to its present location in Hong Kong.

The Indian Army which retained the other 6 regiments of Gurkhas still uses Regimental Depots. The Regimental recruiters bring the new recruits from Nepal to the Depots in India. The Indian Army has approximately 30 Battalions. Terms for enlistment are for 10, 15, or 20 years. A soldier must make corporal to stay beyond 10 years, sergeant to stay beyond 15, and to stay beyond 20 must be a junior commissioned officer (JCO). JCOs can retire at 28 years service or age 50. Pay for an Indian recruit is about 1,000 rupees ($80 US dollars), which is the same pay as Indian soldiers. Riflemens' families normally stay in Nepal, and every two years they get four months leave.

OFFICERS

Commissions in the old Indian Army were from two sources, from the King (Queen) or from a Viceroy. Officers holding them were known respectively as King Commissioned Officers (KCO) and Viceroy Commissioned Officers (VCO). In a British or American battalion, all officers are Second Lieutenants, Lieutenants, Captains, Majors, and so on. In the Indian Army these ranks are assigned only to King's Commissioned Officers, of whom there are about twelve in a battalion. The remaining nineteen officer jobs are carried out by the Viceroy's Commissioned Officers. VCO are not warrant or noncommissioned officers, but officers in the full sense. They cannot, however, command British troops.

Today in the Indian Army they are called Junior Commissioned Officers (J.C.O.) and in the British Army, Queen's Gurkha Officer (QGO). Both JCOs and QGOs are selected, after about fifteen years service in the ranks, from the cream of the Warrant and Noncommissioned Officers. In the British Army exceptional QGOs are made honorary Lieutenants or Captains. To be considered for honorary rank is a singular distinction, and a QGO will only be promoted during his last six months' of service. The number allowed at any one time is rigidly fixed. An increase in pension and respect result from such promotions. (Prior to his retirement Captain Rambahadur Limbu V.C. was promoted to Honorary Captain.)

The QGOs have their own Mess and rates of pay. Lieutenants are platoon commanders while Captains are seconds in command of companies. The Gurkha Major, (one per battalion JCO hold the same positions in the Indian Army) is the second most influential person in the battalion (after the Battalion Commander). He commands nothing and everything. His duties are vague and large, thus permitting him such scope as he desires. The Gurkha Major has no fixed duties other than to advise the commander on strictly Gurkha matters.

Recently some Gurkhas have received the Queen's commission and thus rank with British officers. The senior Gurkha is Lieut. Col. Lalbahadur Pun, of the 2nd Gurkha Rifles, up to now the only Gurkha from Nepal to have attended the Staff College. He was born and educated at Dehro Dun in India, where his father became a Captain QGO in the 2nd Gurkhas. After attending Eaton Hall and Sandhurst, where he finished twentieth out of more than one hundred cadets, he joined the 2nd Gurkhas in 1959. He went with his Battalion to Brunei during the revolt in 1962 and later to Sarawak during the confrontation. LTC Pun was awarded the Military Cross in 1966 for action in Borneo. In 1980 he commanded the Training Depot Brigade of Gurkhas in Hong Kong. Another recent graduate of the Royal Military Academy, Sandhurst (RMAS) was LT Bijay Kumar Rawat, 7th Duke of Edinburgh's Own Gurkha Rifles, who was the first Gurkha officer to be awarded the Sword of Honor at R.M.A.S. as the best cadet of his class. He received the Sword in 1981 from the Supreme Allied Commander Europe, General Bernard Rogers.

LT. Bijay, a line boy, was the son and grandson of Gurkha soldiers. He was born in Malaya, where his father served as Gurkha Major of the Gurkha Signals Regiment. He was educated in Singapore and in Hong

Kong. Bijay had to go to Nepal to enlist when he turned seventeen. After seven years in the ranks, he won an appointment to Sandhurst. Although commissioned a Second Lieutenant upon graduation from the RMAS, he was immediately promoted to Lieutenant for his service in the ranks. Like his fellow British officers, he will have older QGOs under him. In many ways, like all commissioned officers, his future will depend upon them.

British officers for the Brigade of Gurkhas normally come straight from Sandhurst. Some serve in a British Infantry Battalion for a year to get experience before joining a Gurkha Regiment. Two things a British officer must learn: Gurkhali and to eat the native Nepalese food. British officers feel very close to their men. Many could not tell you about British soldiers because they never served with them. That's the way they like it.

FAMILY LIFE OF SOLDIERS

A young Gurkha will serve for a minimum of fifteen years. After his initial three years, he will receive six months leave. During this time many will marry. Wives stay in Nepal while their husbands are with the Regiments. At least once in that fifteen years, his family will be allowed to join him for three years. Then they must return to the hills to give someone else a turn. But if he gains promotion to senior NCO or officer he is allowed to have his family with him.

Although a Gurkha may be betrothed at a very early age, married life does not begin, as a rule, until both boy and girl are at least sixteen years old. Among the Gurkhas, it is the rule rather than the exception for boys and girls to choose their own partners often without the parent's knowledge. Polygamy (now outlawed) was once permitted, and a man could have as many wives as he could afford. The Gurkha is by nature tolerant and fairly easy going. He is an excellent family man. He is a loving father whose family is colorful, cheerful and gregarious. For children living within the Regiment, there is a school staffed by Nepali teachers. The children are taught Nepali and other school subjects, including English. Marriage, however usually does not end casual sexual encounters when his family is back in Nepal.

The Women's Royal Voluntary Service provides each major Gurkha unit with a resident volunteer worker who looks after the soldiers' wives in the sometimes unfamiliar new environment of the Regiment. A family hospital is also provided, under direction of the Battalion's Medical Officer. This is in addition to the Army's normal hospital services.

FESTIVALS

Of the many Hindu festivals which take their place in the Gurkha's year, the Dashera is singularly important. It regulates the whole of a Gurkha's year. The form of its celebration varies slightly in different parts of the country, but the main features are the same. The Gurkha regards it as the warrior's festival, a time to worship Durga and the goddess of Victory and the weapons of his soldier's profession. Dancing and general merry making culminate in the all night celebrations on the night called Kalratri. British Officers and their wives as well as local officials are invited. The entertainment varies according to opportunity and circumstances from the "Penny Gaff" type to more ambitious dramatic performances. But the age old tribal dances are performed; dancers are dressed in Nepali costumes as Pursengis (male dancers) and Marunis (female dancers impersonated by men). These dances go on continuously until on the following day called Mar. Then numerous pigeons, goats and young buffalo bulls are sacrificed at the Maula, a specially selected place of worship near the battalion area. The sacrifice is performed by chopping off the victim's head with a Kukri or Konra. The Konra is a heavy curved weapon with a broad head rough at right angles to the cutting edge. It is always considered a point of pride to sever the head cleanly, with one strike. The rest of the day is devoted to family parties, complete with lots of food and drinks. The festival concludes with the worship performed on the last day known as Tika. Then all men put caste marks on their foreheads. Even if all other festivals are missed, Gurkhas make great efforts to celebrate the Dashera.[39]

WHY GURKHAS ARE GOOD SOLDIERS

The Gurkha is famous as a jungle fighter, yet this is not his natural terrain. He achieves his skill in the jungle through a combination of training and his own natural capacity to make himself an efficient soldier under any conditions. It has been said that a good infantryman should possess the skills of a poacher. The Gurkha learns these skills from his boyhood. Without exception, Gurkhas are highly motivated. They approach soldiering with gusto. Gurkhas are not spoiled by modern comforts, and they are used to physical hardship. They tend to accept things as they are and try to make the best of any situation. When things go wrong, the Gurkhas are uncomplaining. Gurkhas are very loyal to both his fellow soldiers and his unit. Although they often seem slow learners, anything, they learn stays imprinted on the Gurkha's mind and character. He is disciplined without being servile. The Gurkha has a self discipline, beginning with pride in his own achievements. He never thinks of giving up, in sport or combat. Most importantly the Gurkha takes pride in himself, pride that he is a damn good soldier. Gurkhas in general don't work with advance electronic weapons, instead they seek maximum conditioning to be ready to take relatively simple rifles, machine guns and mortars wherever they are needed in a hurry.

THE FUTURE

Speculation on the future of the Gurkha units will continue until the British Government reveals what is to happen to them. In 1997 the Chinese will take over Hong Kong. Since the island and New Territories house the Gurkha Regiments and Training Depot, the Brigade's future is somewhat linked to that of the area. But forecast of doom in 1997 for this tough fighting force which makes up about ten percent of the British Army infantry is premature, to say the least.
The British Parliament has said, "there would be a continuing role for the Gurkhas." Today the Brigade is stationed in Hong Kong, with a battalion in Brunei and one in the United Kingdom. It may have to reduce some of its units through amalgamation. Out there are still areas in which Gurkhas can serve. It would be a big mistake to say that because Hong Kong is gone the brigade is also gone, when there are many places it can be employed to include Europe. The Sultan of Brunei wants a battalion stationed in his country as a deterrent to any would be rebels. Great Britain has commitments to Belize for its defense, where a brigade size Task Force is stationed on a permanent basis. What better place to establish a new home for the Brigade of Gurkhas. The Engineers, Transportation and Signal units would be very much employed. Battalions could rotate for short tours to other duty stations

like Great Britain (2 years), Falkland Islands (1 year) Gibraltar (1 year) and the British bases in Cyprus (1 year). Families could accompany their soldiers when stationed in Belize or Brunei. Even reduced in size, it seems unlikely that there would not be some use in the foreseeable future for such a fighting force.

Why should the Gurkhas be prepared to fight so bravely in a foreign army, in a foreign country? They simply don't look upon the British as a foreign country or being part of a foreign army. They have fought along side British soldiers for Great Britain's causes for so long, that the Army is very much a part of their life, and they look upon the United Kingdom as a second home.

British attachment to the Gurkhas goes beyond active services. Gurkha welfare schemes provide charity grants, training of medical assistants, and educational and economic aid. In addition, Gurkha Welfare Trusts and the British Military Hospitals all work to support the ex-service members and their families. The remittances and pensions paid to the Gurkhas are second only to tourism, as Nepals principle source of foreign currency. It is a measure of Britain's debts to Nepal that each year, 20,000 servicemen or their dependents collect their pensions in the hills.[40]

Field Marshal Slim, the most famous officer of the Gurkhas, wrote: "The almighty created in the Gurkhas the ideal riflemen; he is skilled in the field, on the parade field, and honest in word and deed." What more can he said?

ENDNOTES

1. Graham Smith, "-Farewell V.C. Sahib!," Soldier, The Magazine of the British Army, 22 April 1985, pp. 26-27.

2. The Gurkha Soldier, U.S. Army Military History Institute, Mercenaries File.

3. Colonel R. G. Leonard, Nepal and the Gurkhas, pp. 1-16.

4. Toni Hagen, Nepal The Kingdom in the Himlayas, pp. l00-115.

5. Harold James and Denis Sheil-Small, The Gurkhas, p. 14.

6. Byron Farwell, The Gurkhas, p. 29.

7. James and Small, pp. 16-17.

8. Karl Eskelund, The Forgotten Valley, pp. 57-58.

9. Farwell, pp. 46-47.

10. Farwell, pp. 126-127.

11. History of the 5th Royal Gurkha Rifles (Frontier Force), Vol. 1, p. 253.

12. James and Small, pp. 70-71.

13. John Masters, Bugles and a Tiger, p. 81.

14. Ibid., pp. 81-82.

15. Farwell, p. 87.

16. J.B.R. Nicholson, The Gurkha Rifles, pp. 19-20.

17. James and Small, p. 66.

18. Colonel J.N. Mackay, A History of the 4th Gurkha Rifles, p. 14.

19. Leonard, p. 36.

20. Farwell, p. 100.

21. Philip Mason, A Matter of Honour, pp. 418-21.

22. Byron Farwell, Fierce Johnny Gurkha, pp. 37-41.

23. Shermer, Heifterman and Mayer, Wars of the 20th Century, pp. 221-224.

24. Masters, p. 82.

25. Leonard, pp. 38-39.

26. James and Small, p. 84.

27. LTC. Donald R. Gardner, Britain's Legendary Soldiers, p. 52.

28. Eric Larrabee, Commander and Chief, FDR and His Lieutenants and Their War, p. 561.

29. LTC. H.J. Huxford, History of the 8th Gurkha Rifles, 1924-49, p. 307.

30. History of the Royal Gurkha Rifles (Frontier Force), Vol. II, p. 275.

31. Farwell, p. 257.

32. James and Small, p. 256.

33. Brigadier E.D. Smith, "There Was Much More to it Than That," British Army Review, April 1979, pp. 34-37.

34. Masters, p. 84.

35. The British Army in the Falklands 1982, p. 20.

36. Byron Farwell, Then the Gurkhas Came Ashore, pp. 24-25.

37. Mike Starke, "Tomorrow's Gurkhas in the Making," Soldier, The Magazine of the British Army, June 1978, p. 18.

38. Mike Starke, "Where Life is so Rewarding," Soldier, The Magazine of the British Army, January 1984, p. 25.

39. Robin Adshead, Gurkha, The Legendary Soldier, pp. 119-121.

40. Gurkha Welfare in Action. "Pamphlet of the Gurkha Welfare Trusts."

BIBLIOGRAPHY

1. Adshead, Robin. Gurkha: The Legendary Soldier. Asia: Pacific Press, 1970.

2. History of the 5th Royal Gurkha Rifles (Frontier Force) Vol. 2. (1928-1947) Printed for the Regimental Committee by Gale Polden, Aldershot 1956.

3. Nepal and the Gurkhas. Ministry of Defense, HMSO, London: 1960.

4. The Gurkha Soldier. The Army Military History Institute, Carlisle Barracks, PA.

5. Barclay, CN (ed). The Regimental History of the 3rd Queen Alexandra's Own Gurkha Rifles Vol 2. London: 1953.

6. Burne, Alfred H. LTC. The Art of War on Land. Harrisburg: Stackpole Books, 1966.

7. Bullock, C.J.D. Major. "2/2 Gurkhas Rifles Cross Border Operations." British Army Review, November 1965.

8. Eskelund, Karl. The Forgotten Valley, A Journey into Nepal. New York: Taplinger Publishing Co. Inc., 1960.

9. Farwell, Byron. The Gurkhas. New York: W.W. Norton and Company, 1984.

10. _____. "Fierce Johnny Gurkha." Military History Magazine, December 1984.

11. _____. "When the Gurkhas Come Ashore." Army, September 1982.

12. Hagen, Toni. "Nepal." The Kingdom in the Himalayas. New York: Rand McNally and Co., 1961.

13. Hastings, Max, and Jenkins, Simon. The Battle for the Falklands. New York: W.W. Norton and Company, 1983.

14. Huxford, Harold James. History of the 8th Gurkha Rifles, 1824-1949. Aldershot [Eng] Gale and Polden, 1952.

15. James, Harold and Sheil-Small, Dennis. The Gurkhas. London: MacDonald, 1965.

16. Larrabee Eric. Commander and Chief, Franklin Delano Roosevelt, His Lieutenants and Their War. New York: Harper and Row, Publishers, 1987.

17. MacDonnell, Ranald. A History of the 4th Prince of Wale's Own Gurkha Rifles. compiled by MacDonnell and M. MacAulay 1940-1952, W. Balckwood and Sons, Edinburgh, Scotland.

18. Mason, Philip. A Matter of Honour. (An Account of the Indian Army, its Officers and Men). New York: Holt, Rinehart and Winston 1974.

19. Masters, John. The Road Past Mandalay. New York: Harper and Brothers, 1961.

20. _____. Bugles and a Tiger. New York: The Viking Press, 1956.

21. Morris, John. Hired to Kill. Rupert Hart Davis with Cresset Press, 1960.

22. Nicholson, J.B.R. The Gurkha Rifles. Hippocrene Book, Inc, 1974.

23. Rambahadur, Limbu V.C. My Life Story. (As Told to Warrant Officer Kulbahadur Rai) The Gurkha Welfare Fund, London.

24. Ryan, Denis, George Jocelyn. Historical Record of the 6th Gurkhas Rifles. (1925-1955). Gale Polden, Aldershot, (Eng.) 1956.

25. Shermer, David, et al., Wars of the 20th Century. Secaucus: Book Sales Inc., 1975.

26. Smith E.D. Brigadier. "Friends in the Hills." British Army Review, September 1978.

27. _____. "There Was More to it than That." British Army Review, September 1978.

28. Carleton-Smith M.E. Brigadier. "The Gurkha Field Force." British Army Review, May 1979.

29. Starke, M. "Tomorrow Gurkhas in the Making." Soldier, The Magazine of the British Army, June 1978.

30. Sen-Gupto, Brigadier A.K., India Army. Personal Interview. USAWC: Nov., Dec. 1987.

Printed in Great Britain
by Amazon